DECISION TIME

The Place and Prayer of Surrender

M<small>ARGIE</small> F<small>LEURANT</small>

Copyright © 2015 by Margie Fleurant

Decision Time
The Place and Prayer of Surrender
by Margie Fleurant

Cover photograph by Jon Fleurant www.jonfleurant.com

Printed in the United States of America.

ISBN 9781498429986

All rights reserved solely by the author. The author guarantees all contents are original and do not infringe upon the legal rights of any other person or work. No part of this book may be reproduced in any form without the permission of the author. The views expressed in this book are not necessarily those of the publisher.

Unless otherwise indicated, Scripture quotations taken from the The Holy Bible, New International Version (NIV). Copyright © 1973, 1978, 1984, 2011 by Biblica, Inc.™. Used by permission. All rights reserved.

Scripture quotations taken from the New King James Version (NKJV). Copyright © 1982 by Thomas Nelson, Inc. Used by permission. All rights reserved.

Scripture quotations taken from the King James Version (KJV) – *public domain*.

Scripture quotations taken from the Amplified Bible (AMP). Copyright © 1954, 1958, 1962, 1964, 1965, 1987 by The Lockman Foundation. Used by permission. All rights reserved.

The River Ministries
P.O. Box 287
Martinsville, NJ 08836
margiefleurant.org

www.xulonpress.com

Dedication

I dedicate this book to all who have said yes to God—to all who have decided to follow Jesus and go all the way with Him, even when it meant laying down their own desires to radically and faithfully obey Him.

Contents

Introduction ix

I. The Place of Surrender

Chapter 1: On the Mat 15
Chapter 2: In the Garden 24
Chapter 3: In the Heart 31

II. The Action of Surrender

Chapter 4: Hearing God 41
Chapter 5: Finding Help 58
Chapter 6: Embracing Hope 67

Conclusion 75
Endnotes 77

Introduction

We all experience times in our lives when we sense God leading us deeper into Himself, taking us in new directions, and asking us to surrender once again. These times are so important, because they determine the course of our lives. They are the moments in which we decide whether or not we will say yes to Him and His plans. These significant moments—what I like to call, decision time—is what this book is all about. How do we recognize God's call deeper, and how do we respond?

In these moments, when we hear whispers of our destiny and the great plans God has for our lives, it is easy to feel unqualified or incapable. The good news is, God is not looking for qualified or capable people. He's looking for willing people—for yielded vessels who will allow His Spirit to manifest gloriously through them. After all, if we were capable or qualified on our own, the plans would not be very great. Only by His abundant grace in our lives are we ever capable of living in greatness. What He asks of us is simple obedience. All we need to do to be qualified for His glorious plans is to be willing to say yes and to step out into unknown and sometimes frightening adventures, trusting in His ability and calling instead of our own.

Often, part of saying yes to God's new season includes saying no to some other things, making overdue changes in our lives. Yielding to this pruning is often hard, but the fruit that will come from it makes that painful cutting worthwhile. When we trust Him enough to obey, we will begin to see the desires and dreams we've been treasuring in our hearts begin to bloom. This is what the prophet Hosea promised:

> Sow righteousness for yourselves, reap the fruit of unfailing love, and break up your unplowed ground; for it is time to seek the LORD, until he comes and showers his righteousness on you (Hosea 10:12).

When we live in obedience, He will shower us with His righteousness. God promises that when we say yes to Him, He will reward us for everything we lay down before Him with greater blessings than we could ask or dream. He promises, "If you will give up the toys of the senses, I will give you the riches of My spirit." We may not like the idea of surrender, but we can trust God, in His goodness, to only ask us to give up what isn't His perfect will for us. All He requires is what would hold us back from the fullness of life in Him.

While the world around us tries to convince us the temporal and material pleasures of this life are what matter, the truth is, we are here on earth to fulfill God's plan. He has called us to be co-laborers with Him, building His Kingdom on earth, sharing the truth of the gospel with unbelievers, and bringing the Church to greater maturity. This is what His heart burns for—that all people would know Him and grow into maturity in Him (see 1 Tim. 2:4). To be part of His great plan for the world, we must be people with willing and obedient hearts. Only then will we be able to find our place in His Body and fulfilling our individual calling as part of the greater plan. The question is, are we willing?

When we say yes to His call to surrender, He will stir up the hunger in our hearts for more of Him. We will learn to know Him more deeply and intimately in that brand new place of saying yes to His grand plan. In that new place of wholeness and intimacy, He will be able to lead us into the fullness of destiny. We will discover our part in His plan and begin to walk it out faithfully. He desires to use us to accomplish great things, if only we will say

Introduction

yes to His call. His plan for our lives may not be easy, but it will be great, because through it we will be enacting His eternal plan.

In the first part of this book, we will look at the place of surrender—through a story from my own life, a story about Jesus, and a look into the human heart, where surrender begins. After that, we will consider the action of surrender—including a brief look at how to hear God's voice, the help we have from the Spirit, and the hope that fills our future. Read slowly. Take time to absorb the material and listen to your heart. As you do, the Holy Spirit will lead you and guide you into all truth, showing you what to do with the next phase of your journey on earth.

I
THE PLACE OF SURRENDER

Chapter 1

On the Mat

Three months after my fiftieth birthday, at the end of a workout session, I was laying on my exercise mat, wrestling with denial about my age and the shift I felt in my heart. I could sense God leading me in a new direction, but I did not want to admit it. My children were preparing to leave for college, and I sensed Him calling me back on the road and back into fulltime ministry. This was the first time my birthday had ever bothered me. I had been fine with thirty and forty, but fifty hit me hard, and I was in denial. We had eaten a little birthday cake, but I did not want to celebrate or talk about it. I did not want to face the change I knew was coming. Instead, until that moment, there on my workout mat, I had been in denial about the turning point in my life, destiny, and ministry.

However, the shift had still affected me. I knew God was working in me, "both to will and to do for His good pleasure" (Phil. 2:13 NKJV). I could sense turning and movement in my spirit, but I did not want to look at it or consider it, because I was comfortable. I liked the season I was in, and I did not particularly want a new one. I had imagined this would be a time when I could rest, hang out with friends, and finally have some time to myself. However, God likes to take us right out of our comfort zones and put us in the zone He has planned for us from the very beginning. That is exactly what He began to do on my fiftieth birthday.

My Father was calling me into a new phase of ministry, calling me to dedicate and consecrate my life in a fresh way. It was decision time for me. The question was: Would I say yes? Would I answer His call to mentor the next generation? Would I write the books He had assigned to me instead of living a life of relaxation. Would I say yes to packing my bags and going to the nations of the world? I knew what He was prompting me to do and be, but did I really want that kind of life for my latter years? Did I feel like being maligned or rejected when others disliked it when I moved in a prophetic anointing?

I faced the question of what I was going to do with the remainder of my life. I knew I needed to obey Him; I was born for this time and purpose. But something in me needed to change, and I needed help with that inward change. I wanted to say yes, but part of me was struggling with saying yes—even though I loved God with all my heart and soul. It was decision time for me, and I could hear Him whispering to me: "If you love Me, feed My sheep. If you love Me, equip this next generation. I am calling you. You are right where I need you to be; your whole life has prepared you for this season. Will you follow Me? I want to make you a fisher of people. I want you to call My Church back to Me in the place of prayer. I have watched over you and taught you through the challenges of life. Now you are ready for the new thing I want to bring you into. I need you in this hour, and the time is short. Will you say yes?"

God knows life changes can sometimes be difficult for us, and He takes us at the pace we need, but at some point, we will need to step out of denial, acknowledge what He's doing, and step up to the occasion. For me, that moment came as I lay on my workout mat. I gave in to what He was saying. I surrendered to the call, to the new phase of my latter years.

It was a defining moment for me, a time when the Holy Spirit awakened me to reality. It was as though He shook me out of my slumber and told me, "Rise up! You have to shine. You have to bring forth your destiny." In answer to His call, I decided to accept the change in age and season, whether I preferred it or not. When I did, as I lay there, tears began to roll down the sides of my face. I cried and cried. And in those moments of weeping, God touched my heart and changed the tears from mourning to joy, just like the Scripture says—"...weeping may stay for the night, but rejoicing comes in the morning" (Ps. 30:5). My tears were an outward expression of my yes to God. This internal shift or transformation broke up the fallow ground in my heart, the part of my heart that had been resisting God's plan.

As a result, when I got up off that mat. I was strengthened internally and ready to do the will of God. I had committed to Him, on that mat that day, "Yes, Lord, I will do what You tell me to do. I will make my latter days count. I will go to a new level." He had asked me, as I stared fifty in the face, "Are you going to retire or re-fire?" And at last, I had answered Him. I had resolved to re-fire and to do whatever He would tell me for the rest of my life.

I said yes because I have an intimate relationship with God. I respect Him, honor Him, and glorify Him. He's my friend who sticks closer than a brother, and He knows me better than anybody else. I trust Him. That is why I said yes to Him. And I asked Him to confirm the continued call to ministry in my life by sending someone to help me. I was exhausted from all the ministry office work, as well as the limited traveling I was doing at the time, and I told Him I needed help. Sure enough, soon after, He sent me exactly what I needed—office help and a traveling companion. In this way, He proved to me once again that where He guides He always provides. He is more trustworthy than we know. After all, it's not my ministry; it's His. If He wanted me to go to the next level, He had to provide!

Simply Trust

So much of our reluctance, at times, to surrendering to God hinges on the issue of trust. Because we don't see how it will all work out, we begin to doubt whether His plans are really best. We don't say that, of course, but in our hearts we start to reason and wonder about the wisdom of what we hear Him saying. We think, Why should I do that? It doesn't make any sense to me. It's not what I want to do. Implied in these thoughts is the assumption that we know better than He does and, therefore, we distrust His plans.

The truth is, He knows us better than we know ourselves, and His plans will not harm us. His plans are always for the purpose of bringing us into true prosperity and giving us hope for the future. He is not trying to punish us but is leading us into change, because the old ways will not bring us to the rest and prosperity He desires for us. That is always His purpose, but we usually cannot see how it will work out on the front end. Instead, we need to trust His intentions toward us in order to say yes.

We need to take that leap of faith, because, as Paul said, "We live by faith, not by sight" (2 Cor. 5:7). Living by faith means trusting God more than we trust our perception of our circumstances. This is what Paul meant when he said, "So we fix our eyes not on what is seen, but on what is unseen, since what is seen is temporary, but what is unseen is eternal" (2 Cor. 4:18). When we make the choice to trust God, in the midst of the unknowns, we will find out just how good He is. That is exactly what happened for me.

While I was on the mat, I dedicated and consecrated myself anew to God's purposes for my life. I finally looked at what God wanted me to do and said yes. When I arose from that mat, it set in motion the will of God for my life. Suddenly, the help I needed began to come to me, and people gathered around to support me. Truly, God was providing for all my needs according to His riches in glory (see Phil. 4:19).

If we really understand who our Father is, we cannot fairly say we cannot trust Him. Trust is always possible for the willing. That doesn't mean it won't be difficult or scary at times, but it does mean we can choose to trust Him, despite our fears. When we do, we will see Him come through for us. So many people want God to prove Himself to them before they will trust Him, without recognizing how impossible that is. For Him to prove Himself faithful to us, we must first trust Him and, in obedience to Him, step into a place of need in faith that He will provide. When I said yes to continuing in ministry, not knowing where my help would come from, I stepped into a place of need, by faith, and God met me there with His abundant provision.

The nature of trust is that it is proven through experience. It is always a risk—a risk we say yes to when we accept Jesus as our Lord and Savior. Another word for trust in God is faith, which the author of Hebrews highlighted as the necessary ingredient for pleasing God: "And without faith it is impossible to please God, because anyone who comes to him must believe that he exists and that he rewards those who earnestly seek him" (Heb. 6:11). The risk of trust—surrender in the face of the unknown—is an essential part of what it means to be a follower of Jesus.

The Bible testifies over and over to the faithfulness and trustworthiness of God. When we feel like we have fallen into a dark place and wonder how we will ever get out, God's Word tells us we can trust Him to help us. David testified of his own experience, "He lifted me out of the slimy pit, out of the mud and mire; he set my feet on a rock and gave me a firm place to stand" (Ps. 40:2), and the New Testament tells us He will do the same for us: "God has said, "Never will I leave you; never will I forsake you" (Heb. 13:5). The Bible tells us the truth of who God has been for others and who He will be for us, but we can only experientially know it in our own lives by choosing to trust Him enough to step out in obedience and see how He will provide. Then we will find out the certainty of His promise: "The Lord's unfailing love surrounds the one who trusts in him" (Ps. 32:10).

Here is a great truth of the gospel: When we learn to truly trust in God, Jesus' promise of an easy yoke and light burden will be manifest in our lives. The things that look difficult and scary in the natural will be easy and light in our hearts, because we will have grasped the true substance of trust in our Father, who will never let us down. When that happens, we will be filled with joy unspeakable, no matter our circumstances, and His glory will rest upon us, because we truly believe in who He says He is. This is the key to the life of surrender to God's will. When we choose trust, we will be ready for decision day.

Decision Day

Simply put, decision day is the moment when we face God's nudging in a different direction, and we must decide whether or not we will obey. It is an invitation to a personal renewal or revival, which is nothing more than a fresh level of obedience to God's will for our lives. Decision day is the day we find out He has something more for us, and we get to choose if we will trust Him to lead us yet again.

When I turned fifty, I faced a decision day in my life. It was not the first, and it will not be the last. We all experience decision days many times over in our lives, because the choice to surrender is not a once-and-done deal. Surrender needs to be a daily posture in our hearts. And at these crucial moments of decision, the posture of our hearts will enable us to say yes again, no matter how terrifying it may seem.

Over the years, if I had not made certain decisions in obedience to God's voice, I would not be where I am today. It is that simple. Some of those decisions were small; some were not. Some of those decisions were lifestyle changes, including making changing to my diet and fitness. Others had to do with attitudes, motives, and even friendships. I needed to let go of some friendships, while others were strengthened. Now, I believe I am reaping the fruit of those decisions to obey over the years. Because I made the changes and choices God pointed me toward, I am now experiencing unprecedented favor, anointing, wisdom, and revelation in my life.

Even in the midst of recent difficulties, I have had so much joy that I can honestly say I am the happiest I have ever been. Not long ago, we went eight days without electricity because of a flood, and it was such a happy week for me. We had no electricity, our basement (my office at the time) was flooded, and we lost various possessions to water damage, including about 400 of my books—but I felt infectiously happy.

It was the strangest thing. I don't have an explanation for it, except that God was doing something deep inside my heart and assuring me that although this was currently a small disaster, something good was going to come out of it. In fact, something good did come out of it, because our homeowners insurance reimbursed for the items that were damaged. With that money, we were able to fund a media project He had led me to undertake called "Necessary Truths in Challenging Times." Even though God did not send the flood, He was allowing me to reap righteousness in my life because of my obedience to His will. What a blessing! This is the impact of the decisions we make, for better or worse.

When we take hold of His calling for our lives and say yes to His will, no matter what, He opens the door for us to succeed, and He blesses us with His goodness. When we embrace His dream for our lives, we will find ourselves living in true happiness. We will not comprehend the ramifications of our choices on decision day, but we have the opportunity to say yes in faith. In this way, we add action to our faith and become "doers of the word, and not hearers only" (James 1:22 NKJV).

When I chose to say yes to God's new season for my life at age fifty, I began to enter into a new and greater phase of ministry. I believe the same will be true for any who step out in obedience to God's call. When we face decision day, and God is asking us to embrace a new season, it can often feel frightening or confusing. But we do not need to be afraid, because He is always with us, always leading the way, and His plans for us are always and only good. The same promise God gave to Jeremiah still applies to us today: "'For I know the plans I have for you,' declares the LORD, 'plans to prosper you and not to harm you, plans to give you hope and a future'" (Jer. 29:11).

When God leads us into something new, it will never harm us. It may look different than what we have done before, but that is just a reality of walking with a God who likes to do new things: "See, I am doing a new thing! Now it springs up; do you not perceive it? I am making a way in the wilderness and streams in the wasteland" (Isa. 43:19). God's words to Israel still apply to us today. He loves to bring newness to our lives and stretch us into new adventures with Him. This means, if we want to walk in His will and experience His true prosperity, we must be open to change. It is impossible to be a person of faith while being resistant to change, because resistance to God's will is pride. About the proud, the Bible says, "God opposes the proud but shows favor to the humble" (James 4:6).

True humility manifests in a heart willing to embrace change and the unknown, when God leads, even if it seems frightening or confusing. True humility trusts God more than self, and the reward for it is favor from God. Several times this year, I have awakened with these lyrics running through my head:

Where you go, I'll go.

Where you stay, I'll stay.[1]

God was working in me and preparing for the upcoming change and the need for me, once again, to dedicate my life to Him by saying yes to His will. We don't always know what's coming, but we can trust Him to tell us where to go and what to do. He will prepare our hearts so that, when decision day comes, we can embrace the change He is bringing to our lives. Our faces will turn in His direction, and we will begin to walk into the perfect destiny of God for our lives, which is always far better than we can imagine:

> However, as it is written: "What no eye has seen, what no ear has heard, and what no human mind has conceived"—the things God has prepared for those who love him—these are the things God has revealed to us by his Spirit... (1 Corinthians 2:9-10).

For many of us, it's decision time. These decisions may seem small or large, but either way, they are important. Perhaps God is leading you to say yes to Him regarding an inward attitude of your heart. Maybe He's leading you to embrace a seemingly small lifestyle change, or maybe He's leading you in a new direction in life. All of these changes have the potential for monumental impact in our lives. Sometimes, God knows what we need is a change in our eating or sleeping habits, and these changes are just as significant to our destiny as others. At one time in my life, God spoke to me about this, and I began to work out, because I plan to live a long life and completely fulfill my destiny. To do this, I need to be healthy.

It is so important to listen to His leading in all areas of our lives, whether they seem significant or not, because each of these areas points us toward God's ultimate plan for our lives on earth. In the next chapter, we will consider our great role model, Jesus, who lived out this lifestyle of surrender, even when it cost Him His life.

Chapter 2

In the Garden

Jesus, the Son of God, modeled for us the significance of surrender. Though He was fully God, He was also fully man and, therefore, experienced the need to submit to His Father. Throughout His life, He daily followed God's voice, as He explained in John 5:19: "Very truly I tell you, the Son can do nothing by himself; he can do only what he sees his Father doing, because whatever the Father does the Son also does." Yet we see this submission most starkly in His decision to follow through with dying on the cross. In the Book of Mark's chronicle of Jesus' hours before His trial and crucifixion, we find five important aspects of surrender:

1. The Place of Surrender

Surrender is always connected to a specific place, to a crossroads where we must make a decision. For Jesus, that place of surrender was Gethsemane, the garden where He prayed just prior to His arrest. Mark recorded: "They went to a place called Gethsemane, and Jesus said to his disciples, 'Sit here while I pray'" (Mark 14:32). This was Jesus' crossroads, where He had to decide whether or not He would move ahead into His great purpose.

We all experience crossroads in our lives, some small and some large. There, we are faced with a decision. Sometimes the right choice is obvious; at other times, it is not as clear. But even if we do not know yet exactly what we should do, we can approach God with a submissive heart, committing our lives and choices to His will.

The word Gethsemane means "oil press."[2] In the same way that olives are crushed in an olive press to make olive oil, in the Garden of Gethsemane, Jesus experienced the pressure of the decision. He faced the reality of what was coming, and He submitted to it. We, too, may often feel pressed when at the crossroads of life, because new oil from the Lord is about to be poured out from our lives. All we need to do is surrender to Him in that place of decision and allow Him to make the needed adjustments in our lives.

2. The Anguish of Surrender

When Jesus arrived at the crossroads of His life, where He had to choose to walk forward into His destiny, He experienced great distress and overwhelming sorrow:

> He took Peter, James and John along with him, and he began to be deeply distressed and troubled. "My soul is overwhelmed with sorrow to the point of death," he said to them. "Stay here and keep watch" (Mark 14:33–34).

Jesus was born to go to the cross. He was sent to earth as an intercessor to bridge the gap between God and sinful humanity. This was His life purpose. Yet as He approached His ultimate destiny, He experienced distress in His soul. Though His spirit was willing, His soul was weak and anxious. As He thought about what was coming, He began to be troubled, because He knew what Isaiah had written about Him and the great suffering He was about to endure. Thus, His soul resisted His destiny. The same often happens in our lives. Because of fear, insecurity, or a lack of trust in God, our souls fight against God's will for our lives. Other Bible heroes wrestled with this as well—like Gideon, who hid in fear, and Moses, who was afraid to speak. Yet God empowered these men to resist their soulish fears and surrender to His will.

At Gethsemane, as Jesus faced His destiny, He felt His own inability and weakness, as a man, to fulfill the plan of the Father. Though He was fully God, He was also fully man (see Phil. 2:5–11), and He felt the weakness of His humanity. To His humanity, the idea of dying on the cross felt traumatic and terrifying. He felt the intensity of that hour and the weight of the responsibility He carried. However, His spirit recognized the eternal import of the cross and reminded Him of all whom He would redeem. He understood the impact and necessity of this moment in history. Thus, though He would be tortured and experience separation from His Father (see Mark15:34), He knew He had to consecrate His humanity by choosing to surrender to the Father's will.

3. The Act of Surrender

As Jesus prayed, He fell to the ground in an act of total surrender. "Going a little farther, he fell to the ground..." (Mark 14:35). By falling prostrate before His Father, He signified that He had surrendered in spirit, soul, and body. Though His soul was troubled, His spirit knew what He must do.

4. The Trust of Surrender

After prostrating before His Father, Jesus prayed:

> Going a little farther, he fell to the ground and prayed that if possible the hour might pass from him. "Abba, Father," he said, "everything is possible for you. Take this cup from me. Yet not what I will, but what you will" (Mark 14:35–36).

Here, while admitting His desire for another way, Jesus surrendered fully to the Father and declared His trust in Him. It is significant that in this moment of great pain and anxiety for Jesus, He referred to His Father as Abba, or Daddy. He used the most intimate term, because He fully trusted His Father to take care of Him as He fulfilled His destiny by going to the cross. He knew

His Father loved Him and would not fail Him. Thus, He trusted His Father to raise Him from the dead. This is what Paul meant when he said, "Christ was raised from the dead through the glory of the Father" (Rom. 6:4). Though He lived a perfect life, Jesus could not raise Himself from the dead but faced death trusting His Father to raise Him up.

In the same way, for us, surrender to God at the crossroads of life means trusting Him like a young child trusts her father to catch her when she jumps into his arms. When we know God like that, we will trust Him to work for our best, and we will surrender to His will. We can trust our Father with all our hearts and souls, because He is both the author and the finisher of every person's destiny. He knows the talents and calling He placed in each one of us; He knows the purpose of our lives. And He knows what will truly fulfill us, because as we follow His leading, we will find our greatest place of peace and joy, regardless of our outward circumstances.

This, however, does not mean surrender is easy. Certainly, Jesus did not find it easy, and it is OK that we sometimes struggle with it, too. Adam R. Holtz described the reality and difficulty of surrender in this way:

In the Christian life, surrender usually is a state of spiritual abandonment in which we have let go of our demands and acquiesced to God's work in our lives. But the real challenge lies in getting there! Surrender involves a willingness to accept someone else's terms. In our relationship with God, it means letting go of our "terms" and embracing God's. Jesus' petition in the Garden of Gethsemane is our model: "Not my will, but Yours be done." Only through such prayers of relinquishment can we let go of our stubborn determination to have things our way.[3]

As Jesus showed us, surrender is not always easy, especially when God is asking us to do difficult things. In the beginning, we may beg, pout, cry, and resist, but eventually we need to stop struggling and decide to release it all to the one who knows us better than we know ourselves. We need to say, like Jesus did, "Not my will, but Yours be done."

5. The Empowerment of Surrender

After Jesus prayed, He was empowered with strength to fulfill His destiny. We see this in Jesus' resolute facing of His betrayer at the end of His prayer time:

> Once more he went away and prayed the same thing. When he came back, he again found them sleeping, because their eyes were heavy. They did not know what to say to him. Returning the third time, he said to them, "Are you still sleeping and resting? Enough! The hour has come. Look, the Son of Man is delivered into the hands of sinners. Rise! Let us go! Here comes my betrayer!" (Mark 14:39-24).

What is important to notice is that Jesus did not just pray once and immediately feel empowered. He prayed the same prayer several times. I have found, in my own life, that sometimes I need to pray in surrender more than once before my soul connects with that prayer and aligns in obedience to God's will. When we find ourselves feeling rebellious and considering ignoring God's leading, the best thing we can do is to pray a prayer of surrender over and over until that commitment to surrender in our spirits overwhelms the resistance in our souls.

As Jesus did this, His attitude shifted, and He was able to confidently walk toward His destiny. Thus, He went to the cross, despising the shame of it (see Heb. 12:2). He was obedient unto death, trusting in His Father to raise Him from the dead (see Phil. 2:8). As a result of His surrender and obedience, Jesus was strengthened to endure the cross. And He was ultimately rewarded for His obedience by being exalted to the right hand of the Father and given a name above every other name and all authority in Heaven and earth (see Heb. 12:2; Phil. 2:9; Matt. 28:18). Not only that, but He was rewarded with the joy of the restored relationship between God and humanity—those who are now called His sons and daughters.

The Prayer for Every Believer

The writer of Hebrews described the amazing reality and result of the surrender and obedience in Jesus' life on earth:

During the days of Jesus' life on earth, he offered up prayers and petitions with fervent cries and tears to the one who could save him from death, and he was heard because of his reverent submission. Son though he was, he learned obedience from what he suffered and, once made perfect, he became the source of eternal salvation for all who obey him (Hebrews 5:7–9).

If Jesus, the perfect Son of God, needed to pray in surrender and obedience, all believers will also need to pray like this at certain times in their lives. When God leads us to the place of surrender and asks us to obey His will, the appropriate response is what I call the prayer of dedication and consecration. By praying this prayer, we turn our hearts and will over to God for a fresh time of renewal and consecration. We do not necessarily need to be backslidden to pray this prayer. It is appropriate for all believers at the beginning of a new season. Most of us will pray it at many times in our journey; it needs repeating during the various seasons of our lives. Surrender is a lifelong process, not an instantaneous act. These prayers of surrender will bring us into increasing intimacy with and trust of our Father.

Through the prayer of consecration and dedication, we say, "God I want all of You and all You have for me. I want to fulfill the destiny You have planned for me from before I was formed in my mother's womb." This prayer brings us to a new place of obedience to the will of God. It brings adjustments in the secret place of our hearts and invites God to pour His grace and strength into us to enable us to move into the new season. When we pray the prayer of dedication and consecration, it sets in motion the will of God for our lives and enables us to partner with His greater purposes for this earth.

God has always loved working with humanity to accomplish His will on earth. He could do it all on His own, but He wants us to be involved. He wants us to partner with Him in His love for people and His desire to help them. When we say yes to God's plan and fulfill His greater purpose for our lives, the life of Christ is manifest through us. We find our place in His Body and perform the function we were made for, so that the Kingdom will be established more fully on earth as it is in Heaven.

God has ordained a specific plan for each of us, as part of His plan for the world, and walking in that plan requires our surrender to His will. This is exactly the purpose of the prayer of dedication and consecration. It brings us to the place of absolute surrender, followed by obedience to God's will. It brings us to the place of total reliance on God's strength and strategy, not our own, to accomplish His great plans for our lives. Only He has the power to carry us into our destinies. All He needs from us is hearts of obedience and surrender.

Chapter 3

In the Heart

To live before the Father like Jesus did, with total submission to His will, our hearts need to not only be willing (or submissive) but also obedient. This is the bottom line for whether or not we will live out our destinies. Are we willing to obey at any cost? There is a difference between being willing to go to the gym and actually doing it. But in order to benefit from exercise, I must follow up my willingness with action. In all areas of our lives, when God speaks, our willingness to obey must be coupled with actual obedience. It is like James said, "Faith without deeds is dead" (James 2:26). Paul said it another way: "It is God who works in you to will and to act in order to fulfill his good purpose" (Phil. 2:13). Both the willingness and the action are crucial.

To walk in this dual willingness and obedience, we must see Jesus as not only our Savior but also our Lord. Many believers are tempted to view Jesus primarily as their Savior—the one who rescued them from spiritual darkness and hell—without realizing that also makes Him their Lord—the one who directs their paths and leads them into truth. But we cannot be fully connected to the heart of God without recognizing His lordship over our lives. Saying yes to His gift of eternal life means saying yes to His authority over all we do. He purchased us with His blood, and now we belong to Him. This is not fearful but glorious, because He is the most righteous and loving Lord, and He only tells us to

Decision Time

do what is best for us. He only guides us toward the fulfillment of our destiny.

However, if we are unwilling to give Him lordship of our lives, not just in word but in action, we will miss out on the goodness and blessing of being a surrendered follower of Jesus. Those who truly surrender to Him as Lord of all will experience the richness of His lordship. This is why it is so important. It's not that God is seeking to have power and control over our lives. He's not egoistic like that. Being in control does nothing for Him. Instead, His motive is always love. Like any good parent, He wants us to submit to His leadership in our lives because He knows what is best for us. His decisions for us are always better than our decisions for ourselves, because He is eternally wise and can see into the future.

The question is, as stated previously, will we trust Him enough to allow Him His rightful place as Lord of our lives. He will not force us, and He will not remove His love from us if we say no. But the reality is, we will miss out, by our own choice, on the blessing He has already provided for us, which is waiting for us along the path He is pointing us toward. We cannot see how that will be true, but it will, because He makes good plans for His children. As we travel His road, by faith in His goodness as our Lord, we will discover how true this really is. We will find ourselves progressing, sometimes in very surprising ways, toward the destiny He planned for us from the beginning. And we will find joy in the journey.

However, if we refuse to acknowledge His lordship with actual obedience to His word, we will experience the opposite. The negative and unnecessary things in our lives (those God has asked us to leave behind) will begin to weigh us down. They will hold us back from destiny and may become besetting sins in our lives that eventually disqualify us from our calling. The path of obedience is far better. On that path, we will find greater joy and freedom than we have ever imagined, but it starts with the simple decision to willingly obey.

The prophet Isaiah outlined this truth and the reality awaiting us on the two paths we must choose between.

If you are willing and obedient, you shall eat the good of the land; but if you refuse and rebel, you will be devoured by the sword. For the mouth of the Lord has spoken it (Isaiah 1:19-20).

Often, all God requires of us is simple obedience. We do not need to be incredibly skilled or brilliant. We simply need to be obedient, and He will take care of the rest. As someone once said, "God doesn't call the equipped; He equips the called." Our job is simply to respond to His call, to be faithful in the little things, believing He will keep His promises. Mary Alice Isleib says it so well:

> Obedience is not based on how big or how small the thing is that God is asking us to do. If we don't obey God today, then we won't obey God in the future when He asks us to do something else. To God, obedience is simple obedience, whether it's big or small in man's eyes.[4]

Obedience is obedience, no matter the supposed import of the request. Whether He asks us to send a friend a card or move across the globe, the importance of obedience is the same. And as Isleib points out, it is a practiced response to God's call. Over and over, we have the choice to once again say yes and obey, and the more we do it, the more we will do it in the future. In this way, through obedience, we are building our faithfulness muscles. As we do, it becomes easier to believe and trust and simply obey, based on our growing faith in God's promises. And, of course, He will come through for us. He always does. He loves to exalt those who have faithfully obeyed His word, no matter what it was. He rewards them not only in this life but also in the life to come. He rewards them with true prosperity.

True Prosperity

Many people are driven by the pursuit of happiness, but the truth is, happiness in itself is only a temporary fulfillment, an often fleeting emotion. Thus, the pursuit of happiness is never-ending. Those who seek it must continually find new things or people or circumstances to bring them happiness. This is a counterfeit of God's greater intention for our lives—prosperity of the soul, a state in which we experience happiness in our relationship with Him, regardless of our possessions or circumstances. Some have called this the difference between fleeting happiness, based on outward realities, and ongoing joy, based on inward realities.

If we think our happiness is found in outward things, we will be hesitant to truly submit to Christ's lordship in our lives. We will want to call the shots in order to assure that we can get what we think will make us happy. We will only want to obey God if His word logically aligns with our plan for attaining happiness. The Christian mindset ought to be the opposite. Knowing our true happiness is found in the realities of our inward life with God, we should be eager to obey His leadership in our lives, because we know that obedience is the key to happiness in life, regardless of what's happening around us.

The counter-cultural truth is this: True prosperity is found in listening to and obeying God, no matter what He calls us to do. The most miserable people are not those who say yes to God but those who know what He is saying and chose to go another way. When people make the decision to turn away from what God is saying, they will never find happiness—not unless they return and obey. I have observed some very miserable people who are running from the five-fold ministry call on their lives. They are trying to find fulfillment in other vocations, but the reality is, they will never be fulfilled until they are doing what God has called them to.

I know other people who make a lot of money and point to all their riches as a sign of their success, yet they are miserable, because they have left their first love. Their primary call is to support the Kingdom of God financially, but they have chosen to keep the money for themselves instead.

I once heard Kenneth E. Hagin say, "Some people live and die and never fulfill the first stage of their ministry." This does not just apply to the traditional ministry roles but to all areas of our lives. God has called each one of us to have an impact in a unique way during our lives on earth. Some are called to pastor or prophesy or teach. Others are called to be inventors or doctors or mothers. We each have a unique and significant call that only we can fulfill. The question is simply whether or not we will say yes to that call.

Kathryn Kuhlman, a mighty faith healer and evangelist in the twentieth century, modeled this sort of dedication to God's call. She said:

> Sometimes I may not understand God's dealing in my life, but I know God has a perfect plan and purpose for me. I did not choose the country in which I was born. I had no control of the century in which I would live. I had no choice of sex, for had I been given a choice I would have chosen to be a man. It would be a thousand times easier to stand behind the pulpit and preach the gospel had I been born a man. As a woman I had two strikes against me before I started. Work would have not been nearly so hard, because there is so much prejudice against a woman preacher. But I was not given my choice of sex.[5]

Kathryn often said she died a thousand deaths every time she was about to stand up to minister to the public. Over and over, she consecrated her life to God and stepped out in obedience to His call on her life. As a result, she reaped the blessing of tremendous fruit.

Like Kathryn, I never aspired to be in public ministry. I was shy, insecure, and quiet, yet God called me to prophesy and preach. Surrendering to that call was not easy. He took me through preparatory seasons I did not understand in order to mold me and prune me. Every season in my life had a purpose connected with my call, and my job was to be willing—to keep moving forward at the sound of His voice, whether I understood or not. I just needed to pray, "Lord, not my will, but your will be done in my life." I was scared to preach and to minister as a woman, but like Kathryn Kuhlman, all I needed to do was be willing and obedient to walk in God's will. He did the rest, and He caused me to eat the good of the land (see Isa. 1:19). This is the result that willing obedience will have in our lives.

The Works of the Flesh

For me, as an introvert, my struggle with surrender has tended toward holding back and feeling insecure and afraid of God's call. Like Moses or Gideon, I have sometimes wanted to ask God to send someone else, to find someone more gifted and confident. This is one potential pitfall on the path to surrender. The other potential pitfall is an overconfidence that actually rushes ahead of God in an attempt to make the promises happen. We find an example of this in the apostle Peter, who was quick to assert his ideas and take action instead of waiting for God's precise guidance. It was Peter who, when seeing the glory of the transfigured Jesus, Moses, and Elijah, suggested the disciples build shelters for them (see Matt. 17:4). Peter was eager to obey and receive, but He needed to learn to wait. Turns out, His idea was not at all on God's agenda.

The same could be said for a lot of the church work that goes on in the Body of Christ. Depending upon our personality, it can be easy for us, after hearing a prophetic promise for our lives, to try to make it happen on our own. We offer to build God a shelter for His promise when He is perfectly capable of fulfilling that promise in His own way and time. Any such attempts are labor in vain. They are fleshly works that will not produce eternal fruit or bring us into our destinies. Paul described this sort of striving when he wrote, "The mind governed by the flesh is hostile to God; it does not submit to God's law, nor can it do so" (Rom. 8:7). Human striving and complete surrender have nothing to do with one another. Either we submit fully to God's plan, or we don't.

Before they went to the Garden of Gethsemane, Jesus told Peter and the other disciples to buy swords (see Luke 22:36). Not long after, Judas and the temple guards arrived to arrest Jesus, and His disciples asked, "Lord, should we strike with our swords?" (Luke 22:49). This was a logical question on their part, but it was not what Jesus had in mind. However, Peter did not wait to hear Jesus' answer. He rushed ahead, based on what he thought he knew, and struck off a man's ear (see Luke 22:50; John 18:10). And once again, Peter received a rebuke for his tendency to rush ahead of Jesus' leadership. Knowing this human tendency, the devil often tries to push us into a hurry. He tempts us to move out of faith and into doubt and unbelief, which lead us away from the Holy Spirit's guidance. The more we listen to doubt and unbelief, the harder it is to hear God's voice. This is why patient and trusting reliance on His guidance is so important. Faith never gets in a hurry but waits for God's go.

Fortunately, Peter eventually learned that surrender involves not just submitting to God's will but also waiting for His plan for how to walk that out. In other words, obedience is not just in the big picture, but the little picture, too. It does not mean just saying yes to God's call to a certain career, but also being willing to wait on His timing and provision. The last thing we want to do, like Peter, is accept the call and then attempt to make it happen in our own strength. After all, any plan we can accomplish on our own is far too small for God. But getting in on His far more exciting plan involves the patience of waiting and listening for every step toward the promised end. The psalmist understood this when he wrote, "Some trust in chariots and some in horses, but we trust in the name of the LORD our God" (Ps. 20:7). Likewise, the wise Solomon said, "In their hearts humans plan their course, but the LORD establishes their steps" (Prov. 16:9). Only He is capable of bringing us into our destinies.

When we live for eternity, we will remember that we will give an account for all the deeds we do while on earth. We will live in light of the importance of true surrender and obedience to the will of God for our lives. This, of course, starts in the heart. The first step to knowing whether we are walking in His will is asking Him to search our hearts and convicting us of places where we have followed our own plans, not His:

> Search me [thoroughly], O God, and know my heart! Try me and know my thoughts! And see if

there is any wicked or hurtful way in me, and lead me in the way everlasting (Psalm 139:23–24 AMP).

He will show us where we have gone astray and lead us back to the path of obedience. He will bring us to another decision day and show us the first step toward our calling. All we need to do is willingly obey.

II
THE ACTION OF SURRENDER

Chapter 4

Hearing God

If we want to be fully surrendered and obedient to God's voice, we first need to hear Him speak. About hearing God's voice, Jesus said, "My sheep hear my voice, and I know them, and they follow Me" (John 10:27, NKJV). Fortunately, God made us to be able to hear His voice. It's part of our DNA as humans to be able to communicate with the spirit realm through our human spirits. We are spirits who have souls and who live in bodies (see 1 Thess. 5:23). These three parts are each essential to who we are, yet they are each unique within us and can be divided from each other according to their function (see Heb. 4:12). With our bodies, we contact the physical realm; with our souls, we contact the intellectual realm; and with our spirits, we contact the spirit realm. In this way, we exist in and communicate with these three realms simultaneously.

The most obvious realm to us is the physical realm, what we can see and touch with our bodies. The body is a gift from God, neither good nor bad, but having potential for both. This is why the Bible tells us we must present our bodies to God as living sacrifices (see Rom. 12:1). Our bodies are designed to be subjected to the rule of our human spirits in alignment with the Holy Spirit (see 1 Cor. 9:27). When we live like this, our bodies are a blessing to us. However, if we allow our physical feelings and desires to rule us, we will not be able to walk by faith. This is what Paul meant when he said we must live by faith and not by sight (see 2 Cor. 5:7). For faith to rule, the physical reality must be subjected to the spiritual reality.

The soul expresses itself through our thoughts, emotions, and human will. It is the conscious part of us, and it strives to guide our lives through logic and emotion. This is why the Bible specifically talks about saving our souls: "Therefore lay aside all filthiness and overflow of wickedness, and receive with meekness the implanted word, which is able to save your souls" (James 1:21, NKJV). In other words, we must submit our souls to the council of the Word of God, which will overcome the wicked nature and replace it with heavenly wisdom.

When saved and aligned with the spirit, the soul can be a powerful tool for right living. A big part of this is changing the way we think, as Paul talked about in Romans 12:2:

> Do not conform to the pattern of this world, but be transformed by the renewing of your mind. Then you will be able to test and approve what God's will is—his good, pleasing and perfect will.

When our minds are renewed, we begin to think in line with the Word of God. Though many Christians continue to live with minds easily tossed about by emotions and ideas, we don't have to live that way. God promises, if we invite Him, to restore and renew our souls (see Ps. 23:3).[6]

The human spirit is the born-again part of our natures (see 2 Cor. 5:17–21; John 3:3–8). The Bible sometimes refers to it as our innermost being or inner person (see John 7:37–39). Solomon said, "The human spirit is the lamp of the LORD that sheds light on one's inmost being" (Prov. 20:27). As the "lamp of the Lord," it comes to life when we accept Jesus as our Lord and Savior. This is why our bodies and souls need to be submitted to our spirits. But like our souls, our spirits also need to be developed and honed by the Word of God (see John 14:26). As our bodies and minds benefit and progress from physical and mental exercise, so do our spirits grow through practicing spiritual exercise. The more we use our spirits and intentionally work on hearing God's voice, the more clearly we will be able to understand Him. If we are eager to hear God's voice, we can, because that is how He made us. However, one key ingredient, when missing, can stunt our growth in hearing God's voice.

The Key Ingredient

Sadly, many believers struggle to hear His voice. Often, that is because they have never been taught to hear God's voice or because they have not fully surrendered. This is the missing key ingredient, causing their resistance to what He might say to block their ability to hear. As disciples of Jesus, we should desire to obey God fully, just like He did. The Old Testament hero, Caleb, is a great example of one who lived to hear and obey God's voice, even if it meant facing the giants in the land. And God rewarded Him accordingly:

> But because my servant Caleb has a different spirit and follows me wholeheartedly, I will bring him into the land he went to, and his descendants will inherit it (Numbers 14:24).

Unlike Caleb, many Christians want to follow God's will, but they have not fully surrendered in their hearts. As a result, they have difficulty distinguishing His voice and knowing whether an idea is from Him or from their own souls. They struggle to identify His plan for their lives and lack the fullness of joy that comes with walking in God's will. The solution to this dilemma is simple—the prayer of dedication and consecration. Having a willing and obedient heart positions us to hear God's direction clearly.

When we pray from a place of surrender, we come to Him without preconceived ideas about what His plan must look like. We simply ask, "What is Your plan for my life? Which way should I go?" When we ask these questions with willingness in our hearts to obey, no matter what He says, we will be able to sense His leading. Praying like this also helps to clarify where an idea or plan is coming from—either from God, our soulish natures, or our selfish ambition and pride. As we pray the prayer of dedication and consecration, the origin of our desires will become clear. The will of God for our lives will be set into motion, and our inner person will gain the ascendency, bringing us to a place of rest.

Now that we know the importance of a surrendered heart to our ability to hear God's voice, we will examine some of the most common ways God speaks to us.

How He Speaks

1. The Inward Witness

The primary way God leads His children is through the inward witness (see Rom. 8:14). As Paul said, "The Spirit himself testifies with our spirit that we are God's children" (Rom. 8:16). We can imagine this witness as an internal traffic light that gives a check (red light) or a good feeling (green light) in our spirits. We don't hear this guidance with our physical ears, but sense it with our inward spiritual intuition. It is hard to describe what this feels like, but the more a person experiences it, the more that person will recognize it. The inward witness isn't a voice; it is an inward intuition or knowing. We just know that we know that we know. I often describe the red light as an illogical premonition and the green light as an illogical velvety feeling. These feelings may not make sense to our minds, because they come from the spirit, not the soul. Our heads may say one thing while our hearts say another.

This is why it is so important for us to spend time alone with God in secret prayer. As Jesus said: "When you pray, go into your room, close the door and pray to your Father, who is unseen..." (Matt. 6:6). When we shut out the distractions of life for a period of focused prayer, we will be able to hear God clearly in our spirits. This means quieting our thoughts and emotions so we can more fully commune with God. Practicing this regularly will give us great sensitivity to the inner traffic light, and we will be able to quickly discern that yes or no in our spirits.

Of course, hearing from God is not a formula, and at times, I have spent quality time in secret prayer regarding direction for a particular decision, yet received no inner witness. Early in my walk with God, I learned that straining to hear God is not very productive. At such times, it is best to leave my place of secret prayer and simply go about my day, while continuing to look inward to see whether I will sense anything from Him in my spirit. Sometimes the witness I did not receive in the prayer closet will begin to take shape as I go through my day. I test it by thinking about it. If I keep getting the same internal witness when I think about the decision, then I follow the witness. Sometimes I wait a few days or weeks to make sure it is the same witness on the inside. One way or another, if we keep our hearts tuned toward our Father's voice in our inner person, we will eventually sense a red or green light.

Some people only want to hear God in spectacular ways, like dreams and visions, but the truth is, God's supernatural presence is with us and guiding us at all times. We just need to quiet down and learn to hear His whisper. When we know His whisper, He can lead us gently:

> I will instruct you and teach you in the way you should go; I will counsel you with my loving eye on you. Do not be like the horse or the mule, which have no understanding but must be controlled by bit and bridle or they will not come to you (Psalm 32:8–9).

If we require loud guidance, we are like brute animals who need to be led by force. Instead, we should be so surrendered to and in tune with God that we respond to His whisper.

Our value should never be found in receiving prophetic words or spectacular visions; our value is always and only found in the fact that we are beloved children of God. It is that simple: "For you are all sons of God through faith in Christ Jesus" (Gal. 3:26 NKJV).

Because we are His children, we can and should hear His voice. This is part of our inheritance in Him: "For those who are led by the Spirit of God are the children of God (Rom. 8:14).

What this means is that using an outward sign or test, some people call them "fleeces," is unscriptural under the new covenant. Under the old covenant, people sometimes needed to use tests to discern God's will, because He did not speak to everyone as He does now. About this coming shift, in the new covenant, God said:

> I will give you a new heart and put a new spirit in you; I will remove from you your heart of stone and give you a heart of flesh. And I will put my Spirit in you and move you to follow my decrees and be careful to keep my laws (Ezekiel 36:26–27).

In other words, since God now speaks to each of us in our hearts, fleeces are no longer a legitimate way to discern His guidance. Some people chose to rely on outward signs, so-called opened and closed doors, rather than taking the time to hear God in their hearts. But relying on outward circumstances can be dangerous, because the devil can open and shut doors, too. The Holy Spirit does not work by a hit-or-miss strategy. He has placed His Spirit inside us so we can hear Him with incredible accuracy. If we spend enough time talking to God, we will know on the inside how He is leading us.

It is also important to remember that God often leads us step-by-step, not leap-by-leap (see Ps. 18:28–36). Through the inner witness, we can sense the right direction for our next step, but we do not see the whole path or even the end result. Following God's voice this way requires patience, but the reward is the intimacy of God's guiding hand. As Psalm 37 says, "The LORD makes firm the steps of the one who delights in him; though he may stumble, he will not fall, for the LORD upholds him with his hand" (Ps. 37:23–24). King David lived in this reality, which he described beautifully in Psalm 23:

> The LORD is my shepherd, I lack nothing. He makes me lie down in green pastures, he leads me beside quiet waters, he refreshes my soul. He guides me along the right paths for his name's sake. Even though I walk through the darkest valley, I will fear no evil, for you are with me; your rod and your staff, they comfort me (Psalm 23:1–4).

As we see in David's experience, the fact that we have direction from God doesn't mean it will be smooth sailing. Jesus told Peter to come, but when Peter looked at the wind and waves, he began to sink (see Matt. 14:25). Likewise, we will often experience turbulence when we walk in step with God's leading. That does not mean we are on the wrong path. When we feel the inner witness from God, we must act on it, regardless of the circumstances. God will always meet us along the path.

I have experienced this in my own life many times. At the end of my two years at Rhema Bible Training Center, a friend of my roommate invited me to visit New Jersey. In response to her invitation, I traveled to New Jersey and did a three-day conference for her. During that time, we became friends, and I returned to New Jersey on several other occasions to minister and to visit.

Meanwhile, I remained in Tulsa, Oklahoma, working at a church and cleaning the house of the lead pastors. As time went on, however, I started to feel bored and dissatisfied. I sensed it was time for a change. I didn't know how God was leading me or how to pray about this inward dissatisfaction, so I simply prayed: "Father God, go before me and prepare the way" (see Isa. 40:3–5). After I prayed everything I knew to pray in English, I would then pray in tongues (we will talk more about this kind of prayer later).

I was single at the time, so I would make dates with God, walk the floors of my rental, and just pray. My prayer focus at that time was for His leading for the next season of my life. Meanwhile, my friendship with this woman and her family continued to grow. I found myself thinking, So many doors are opening up in New Jersey, and I keep going back there. Why don't I just move there? On one of my visits, after praying for direction, I looked in my heart and said, "God, do You want me to move here?" As I pondered that question in my heart, I had a velvety feeling inside, a green light. I vividly remember thinking, I fit in here; I belong here. It was a perfect example of the concept explained in Proverbs 16:

> Roll your works upon the Lord [commit and trust them wholly to Him; He will cause your thoughts to become agreeable to His will, and] so shall your plans be established and succeed (Proverbs 16:3 AMP).

God used my thoughts to confirm His leading in my life. So, I returned to Tulsa, packed up my belongings, and drove to New Jersey—happy about my decision and knowing I had heard from God.

After just a few months in New Jersey, many speaking engagements on the East Coast began to open for me. One church I spoke at in Pennsylvania asked me to help them pioneer their church, while also continuing to travel to other churches. I agreed, and in haste, I packed up my car and headed to Pennsylvania. The day I arrived, the pastor and his wife invited me over for lunch. As I walked up to their house, I felt a sudden premonition in my spirit, and I thought, What have I done? I felt a heavy weight on the inside. It was not at all like a velvety feeling in my spirit. Immediately, I knew I had made a mistake. And as it turned out, I was with that church for less than six months. Afterward, I moved to join another church in Pennsylvania, and eventually, I moved back to New Jersey.

God has a plan for our lives, and He wants us to be surrendered and committed to His plan. At times, even though our hearts are right, we will make mistakes. It's like driving a car to a destination. If I am on the road heading to a certain destination, following my GPS, but I miss the turn I'm supposed to take, the GPS will always recalculate the route and take me to my destination via a different route. It may take a little longer, but eventually I will get to the right destination. At times, our journey of surrender and commitment to the will of God works like this. Even though I mistakenly moved to Pennsylvania, I eventually found my way in that season.

Now, every time I sense God leading me into something new or different, I go to the place of secret prayer, surrender my will to Him, and say, "Lord, what are You saying to me? What do You want me to do? Where are you leading me? What is Your plan?" And then I wait until I know that I know and have the inward witness. When we ask these questions with willingness in our hearts to obey, no matter what He says, we will be able to sense His leading. Praying like this helps to clarify where an idea or plan is coming from—either from God, our soulish natures, or our selfish ambition and pride. As we pray the prayer of dedication and consecration, the origin of our desires will become clear. The will of God for our lives will be set into motion, and our inner person will gain the ascendency, bringing us to a place of rest.

2. The Rhema Word

Simply put, a rhema word is when the Holy Spirit uses the written Word of God to speak specifically to a person's life situation. This happens when I am reading the Bible, and suddenly a verse seems to jump out at me, and God uses it to give me direction for my life. It is not necessarily the meaning of the verse in context, but it is what God is speaking in that moment through the verse. This is possible because the Scripture is alive and active (see Heb. 4:12). Through it, God can speak to us regarding direction for our lives. When He does, our hearts will witness that it is God's voice guiding us through these verses. Of course, we must remember that the Word of God is the final authority on how to live life; any rhema word we receive from God will align with the Bible. If it doesn't, it's not from Him.

Rhema words are important because the Bible does not always give us insight on specific direction for our lives. It doesn't tell us where to move or what job to take or the answers to a myriad of other questions for our individual lives. In Mark 16:15, Jesus commanded us, "Go into all the world and preach the gospel to all creation." This is a universal command for all followers of

Jesus. The question is, what does it look like for each one of us? For some people, it means moving across the world; for others, it means sharing Jesus in their workplace and neighborhood. The Bible doesn't tell each one of us how this verse should be applied in our lives, but the Holy Spirit will guide us with wisdom and direction.

Even in the lives of the early apostles, who received this command from Jesus in person, we see that it was applied in different ways (see Acts 13:2-4). We find an interesting story about this in Acts 16, where Paul was planning to take the gospel to Asia, but the Spirit forbad them from going there and sent them to Macedonia instead (see Acts 16:6-10). Here, even though the Word of God says go, the Spirit told Paul not to go one place and to go another instead. In other words, we need both the general guidance of the Scripture and the specific application of the Scripture that the Holy Spirit shows us. The rhema word is a common way in which God speaks to us. When we pray from the place of surrender, God loves to direct us through His rhema word.

3. The Inward Voice

Each part of our beings has a voice. The feelings are the voice of the body, the reason is the voice of the soul, and the conscience is the voice of the spirit. Paul referred to the spirit in this way when he said, "I speak the truth in Christ—I am not lying, my conscience confirms it through the Holy Spirit" (Rom. 9:1). The inward person, the human spirit, has a voice just as the outward person has a voice. We call this voice the voice of our conscience, or the still small voice. In this way, our spirits—which are the Lord's lamp into our inward selves—will speak to us.

Because our spirits are made alive in Christ, we can trust them and should always listen to them (see 2 Cor. 5:17). We see an example of this in the life of Paul: "Paul looked straight at the Sanhedrin and said, 'My brothers, I have fulfilled my duty to God in all good conscience to this day'" (Acts 23:1). Our consciences are good guides, because they are filled with the Holy Spirit. We can trust and depend upon them, knowing our spirits recognize realities our heads cannot comprehend. When we rely on the inward voice of our spirits, we become God inside–minded (see John 14:23; 1 Cor. 3:16; 2 Cor. 6:16).

Not long ago, I experienced this in a powerful way. I still live in New Jersey, but I also regularly travel to my Florida home to study my Bible, pray, and write. On one of those trips, I had planned to have five days alone, because I was expecting it to take some time for me to hear from God. However, on the first morning, as I walked into my kitchen, I heard a still small voice on the inside of me. It said one word: pioneer. I opened my journal and wrote it down. Then I heard, "You are going to pioneer a movement." Again, I wrote it down, feeling both puzzled and reluctant.

What I heard wasn't a loud voice, but a still small voice; yet the sound was very clear. It was like it had gently bubbled up from my innermost being and entered my thoughts. Then, the morning after He spoke this to my heart, God confirmed what I had heard through two trusted individuals in my life, who both had visions about me. I received no other immediate direction, and He did not give me further details about this movement I was to pioneer. For the rest of those five days, I heard nothing else from God. Even though I didn't yet understand all the implications of what He had said, I knew I had heard Him speaking inside me.

4. Voice of the Holy Spirit

The inward voice of the Holy Spirit, speaking to our spirits, is not the same as the still small voice, which is the voice of own spirits speaking to us. When the Holy Spirit within speaks, it is more authoritative. After Peter saw a vision, the Spirit spoke to him, telling him what to do next: "While Peter was still thinking about the vision, the Spirit said to him, 'Simon, three men are looking for you'" (Acts 10:19). The voice of the Holy Spirit often feels so real, although it is internal, that it can cause us to look around to see who spoke, just as Samuel did (see 1 Sam. 3:1–10). When the Holy Spirit speaks to us, it is usually more spectacular than the inward voice of our spirits, and it often indicates difficult times ahead. The good news is, the Holy Spirit sees what we're heading into, and He comes to prepare us by speaking directly to us.

Jesus had the Spirit without measure—not only upon Him but within Him (see Luke 4:1, 14, 18–21). The Holy Spirit was at work in Jesus' life and ministry, and when Jesus faced His ultimate purpose for coming to the earth, the Holy Spirit strengthened Him and led Him into His destiny. He does the same for each one of us. As born again children of God, we too are filled with the Spirit of God and can walk as closely with Him as Jesus did, following His every move. And that should be our goal.

Of course, it is important to mention here the need to test everything we hear. None of us hear perfectly, and if we are not careful, we can be deceived by demonic voices masquerading as angels of light. This is why we must always test everything we hear against the Word of God. As Paul said, "Do not treat prophecies with contempt but test them all; hold on to what is good" (1 Thess. 5:20–21). The Holy Spirit will never say something to us that contradicts what He has already said in the Bible. Thus, we must weigh each word from God against the entire witness of the Bible, discarding any words that contradict it. While the Bible is not the only way God speaks to us, it is the standard. It contains all we need to be faithful followers of God. This means we do not need to seek after voices or wrestle to hear something from God (see 1 Cor. 14:10). He is not a puppet who speaks on command. Yet He loves to speak to His children. When we are content in Him and committed to His Word, we can trust that He will speak to us. The danger comes in striving to hear something right away instead of waiting on God's timing. Remember, we can also learn just as much from what God doesn't say as from what He does say.

Once I heard the Holy Spirit speak during an extremely painful and difficult time in my life. I had made an important decision that had led me right into difficulty because I thought it was the right choice and God was leading me. As a result, over and over, I would question my intuition. I began to wonder if I had missed God and if I had made the right choice. I wondered, If I had heard from God, wouldn't it be easy? One morning, as I was thinking about how difficult things had become, I heard the Holy Spirit say inside me, "Are you willing to trust Me?"

I knew it was God, and I knew exactly what He was referring to. I said, "Yes, Lord, I am." I knew He knew what was best for me, and if I followed Him—even in the midst of the difficult circumstances—everything would work out, not just according to His plan but also according to what was best for me and the call of God on my life . In that moment, I chose trust and surrender. A few months later, at a women's conference, the speaker gave me a word of prophecy: "Margie, I don't know what this means, but God wants you to know that you didn't make a mistake." I knew exactly what God was saying; He was referring to the decision I had made and then doubted. This word confirmed, again, that I could trust God's guidance and that, even though my circumstances seemed to deny it, I had heard and followed God's leading correctly. We can trust the voice of the Holy Spirit.

5. Perception

Perception is similar to the inward witness. We find an example of perception in the story of Paul's shipwreck at sea. Before the ship set sail, Paul perceived that the journey would be disastrous:

> Much time had been lost, and sailing had already become dangerous because by now it was after the Day of Atonement. So Paul warned them, "Men, I can see that our voyage is going to be disastrous and bring great loss to ship and cargo, and to our own lives also (Acts 27:9–10).

He did not know this because of a great revelation or even because the Lord told him. He simply perceived it in his spirit.

6. Spectacular Guidance in Visions

While God often guides us and speaks to us through the more subtle methods we've already discussed, sometimes He also uses dreams and visions to speak to His children (see Joel 2:28). Visions are not an everyday occurrence, yet those that are recorded in the New Testament provided significant direction for believers (see Acts 10: 1–7, 9–10; 19:12–20; 26:19). Though we should never seek after visions and dreams, we should always be receptive and take them seriously if they come. Because dreams and visions are often partially or fully symbolic (see Acts 11:1–12), we need diligence and wisdom to interpret them. Often, as we pray about what we have seen, we will receive understanding through our spirits or the Holy Spirit.

In the Bible, we see three basic types of visions—a spiritual vision, a trance, and an open vision. First, a spiritual vision is seen with the eyes of the spirit. For example, in Acts 9:8, when Saul encountered Jesus on the road to Damascus, his physical eyes were blinded, yet he was able to see a vision of Jesus with his spiritual eyes. Second, a trance is a sort of vision in which all physical senses are suspended, and the person is more conscious of the spiritual than the physical and often does not know what is happening around him or her. We find an example of a trance in Acts 10:9–11, where Peter saw a sheet full of animals coming down from Heaven. Third, in an open vision, the person's eyes are open and physical senses are intact, yet the person is seeing into the spiritual realm (see Acts 9:10–12).

7. Spectacular Guidance by Prophecy

Another way God sometimes speaks is through prophecy. The apostle Peter gave us this simple definition of prophecy: "For prophecy never had its origin in the human will, but prophets, though human, spoke from God as they were carried along by the Holy Spirit" (2 Pet. 1:21). In other words, prophecy happens when a person hears a message from God for another person or a group of people and shares that message by the Holy Spirit. We find examples of this throughout the Bible, and the New Testament shows prophecy as an important part of the early Church (see Acts 13:1; 15:32; 21:8–14; 1 Cor. 12–14; 1 Tim. 4:14).

In the last one hundred years, the Church has grown tremendously in its understanding of the supernatural, including the gift of prophecy. With this increase of knowledge has come an increase in desire. People are hungry for the prophetic, and as a result, they are beginning to hear God more. However, the potential pitfall in this hunger is the tendency to look to prophecy and those who prophesy as our primary source of God's voice. Prophecy is such a gift for encouragement, edification, and comfort (see 1 Cor. 14:3), but it is only one way we hear God speak. It is dangerous to spend our lives seeking out prophecies, just as it is dangerous to build our lives upon prophesies.

Instead, we must seek God and build our lives upon His word (see Matt. 7:24–25), no matter how it comes to us. When people prophesy to us, our spirits should bear witness to the words. If a prophecy does not resonate with our spirits, chances are the prophecy is wrong. As new creation believers, we are not dependant on the man or woman of God to hear God's voice for us. Now, we all have the Spirit of God living within us and are able to hear Him for ourselves. This means, if what someone else is saying does not align with what we sense in our spirits, we are not obligated to submit to that person's prophecy. We submit to God alone, trusting Him to guide us into His perfect path for our lives. As we keep our hearts pure and teachable before Him, He will guide us and show us when we are wrong. Prophecy is intended, in the New Covenant, as a source of strengthening and encouraging along our journeys. But it should not replace our responsibility to hear from God for ourselves.

Likewise, when prophecies speak of future events, we must be careful not to try to make those events happen on our own strength. If God wants us to participate in fulfilling a prophecy, He will speak to us clearly about the part we play. Then, our job is simply to obey what He has said and trust the rest of it to Him. He will bring it to pass as we wait on His timing, which is often very different from our own. Some prophecies may take years to be fulfilled, but if we wait on God's timing, we can trust Him to fulfill them just as He has promised.

I have received and given many prophetic words over the years I have been a Christian. One particular prophecy I received came after I had lived in Pennsylvania for some time and was praying about moving back to New Jersey. While I was at a conference, the speaker called me up and sang a prophetic word over me: "You've said, 'Lord, I will go wherever You lead me. I will follow You, Lord, wherever You want me to go.' Days are approaching now when you'll tap into a greater source of power than you've known before, and your life will grow and glow. In three months, you will see a tremendous change. A tremendous change is coming into your personal life and your ministry. You've prayed for it, you've seen it, and I've shown it to you. Now you will go in and go through that open door...."

This prophetic word confirmed the desire in my heart and the leading of God to return to New Jersey. Within three months, I moved back to New Jersey, and I also met my future husband. This example shows us how God can use prophecy to guide us along His path for our lives—when prophecy is in agreement with the Scripture and with the inner witness in our spirits.

This survey of seven ways God speaks just scratches the surface. Many books have been written on the subject of hearing God's voice.[7] The important point is this: We can hear God speak. And, He wants to speak to us. When we really understand these truths, we will find ourselves on a grand adventure into the heart of God, guided by His Holy Spirit. The more we respond in openhearted obedience, the more we will hear His voice.

It is not difficult to be led by the Holy Spirit. If we are honest with ourselves and honest with God, our thoughts and desires will begin to align with His thoughts and desires.

> The plans of the mind are orderly thinking belong to man, but from the Lord comes the (wise) answer of the tongue. All the ways of a man are pure in his own eyes, but the Lord weighs the spirits (the thoughts and intents of the heart). Roll your works upon the Lord, (commit and trust them wholly to Him; He will cause your thoughts to become

agreeable to His will, and) so shall your plans be established and succeed (Proverbs 16:1–3 AMP).

As this passage shows, self-awareness is crucial to our ability to hear God and obey His leading. Though we do not always understand the motives of our hearts, God does, and if we are willing, He will show them to us and help us align our hearts with His motives. When I face decision day, I pray like this: "Lord give me the wisdom to discern what is in Your heart and mind and what is in my own heart and mind." Often, this is exactly what happens when we face a decision day and God asks us to let go and trust Him in simple obedience. Hearing His voice is the first step; obeying is the second.

Fortunately, though this can feel daunting, we are not alone. When Jesus left this earth, He promised to send the Helper to assist His disciples in their mission on earth. In the next chapter, we will see how the great Helper is available to assist us in the call to surrender and obedience.

Chapter 5

Finding Help

When Jesus first told the disciples about the coming Spirit, He referred to the Spirit as the Helper (see John 14:16, 26; 15:26; 16:7 NKJV). In this, He showed the Spirit's primary function in our lives. He assists us in our new creation living, empowering us to be holy and obedient to God. Jesus also promised the Helper would abide with us forever, remind us of His words, and testify about Him. This is good news! We are not responsible, on our own strength, to obey God's leading. In our humanity, we are incapable of living the way God wants us to live. That is why He has made us new creations and filled us with His Spirit, who enables us to live righteously.

Thus, the Holy Spirit helps us when we pray the prayer of dedication and consecration, when we surrender our lives anew to God's will. Though it may feel scary to surrender, we can be reassured by the Holy Spirit's presence with us. He is here to help. Our obedience is "...'Not by might nor by power, but by my Spirit,' says the LORD Almighty" (Zech. 4:6). I am so glad Jesus did not leave us alone on earth. He did not put the full responsibility of fulfilling our destiny into our hands but promised to help us obey His call and impact the world for His Kingdom. We are never alone on the journey. Therefore, no task is too difficult for us.

With the Holy Spirit living inside us, we can face any dilemma. When we don't know what to pray, He helps us. When we don't know what to do, He guides us. When we emotionally have run out of strength, He is there to strengthen us. We are not alone. And, as the apostle John reminded us, "...the one who is in you is greater than the one who is in the world" (1 John 4:4). In the rest of this chapter, we will be looking at two ways the Holy Spirit is our Helper—in our obeying and in our praying.

Help with Obeying

It all starts with the Spirit, our great Helper. We are His temples, and through us, His will is accomplished in our lives. God promised the Israelites that some day He would live inside them; we now live in that reality, as the apostle Paul pointed out:

> ...We are the temple of the living God. As God has said: "I will live with them and walk among them, and I will be their God, and they will be my people" (2 Corinthians 6:16).

As we fully surrender to Him, we make a way for our spirits to have precedence over our minds and emotions. This enables a greater level of obedience in our lives and facilitates the fulfillment of our destinies. We all desire His lordship in our lives, but we don't always know how to walk it out. The Holy Spirit helps us make this desire a reality, enabling us to live in the fullness of who God created us to be. As Jesus told His disciples:

> ...I am telling you nothing but the truth when I say it is profitable (good, expedient, advantageous) for you that I go away. Because if I do not go away, the Comforter (Counselor, Helper, Advocate, Intercessor, Strengthener, Standby) will not come to you (into close fellowship with you); but if I go away, I will send Him to you (to be in close fellowship with you).... But when He, the Spirit of Truth (the Truth-giving Spirit) comes, He will guide you into all the Truth (the whole, full Truth). For

He will not speak His own message (on His own authority); but He will tell what ever He hears (from the Father; He will give the message that has been given to Him), and He will announce and declare to you the things that are to come (that will happen in the future) (John 16:7, 13 AMP).

As we listen to Him, He tells us the truth about our destinies. He also (as we mentioned in the last chapter) tells us the truth about our motives. As we surrender to what He says, He will help the three parts of our beings (spirit, soul and body) to align with the perfect plan of God for our lives. If these three parts of us are in conflict with each other, we will have difficulty consistently obeying God's will. We will be torn between the guidance of the Spirit and the pull of our minds and emotions. However, when our human spirits (submitted to the Holy Spirit) rule our souls and bodies, we are able to live from the reality of the spirit realm. As new creations, that is our true home, with God in heaven. We are now seated in heavenly places with Jesus (see Eph. 2:6). As a result, the spiritual realm should be more real to us than the natural.

When it is, we will live with the awareness that all we do on earth is being recorded in heaven and that heaven holds the wisdom we need to succeed during our temporary journey on earth. With this perspective, we will be able to truly live for eternity and avoid being driven by daily circumstances or the desires and disappointments of life. We all experience good and bad in this life, but those realities do not have to rule us if we are living from the spiritual realm. Instead, we will be able to rise above our circumstances and see from God's perspective. We will be able to obey His will, no matter what is happening around us, because we know His truth is more enduring than the details of our earthly lives.

When we have a heavenly perspective, we will learn to ask the Holy Spirit to guide us in the midst of every situation. We will learn to see every life decision as part of our calling to bring heaven to earth:

> So He said to them, "When you pray, say: Our Father in heaven, hallowed be Your name. Your kingdom come. Your will be done on earth as it is in heaven" (Luke 11:2 NKJV).

The Holy Spirit will always lead us into the perfect will of the Father for our lives. We only partially know our destinies and the paths to take, but He sees it all. He knows all about our lives, from the moment we are born till our last breaths. He is both the author and the finisher of the plans He has for us. He wrote the script of our destinies, and through His Spirit, He acts it out in our lives. Because of this, life lived by the Spirit can often seem like a good mystery book. Just when we think we have it all figured out, we find another clue. And off we are again, on the grand adventure into our calling.

I have experienced this over and over in my own life. One of the most significant "clues" surfaced in 1981, when God sent me to the East Coast to begin full-time ministry. Within four years, I had a full-time assistant and two friends who traveled with me part-time. The ministry was exploding, and many people were being touched by God. Yet, we knew this was only the beginning. We sensed God wanted to do a new thing and take us to the next level. It was a decision day for us, and we said yes to all He had for us. My two friends, my assistant, and I dedicated our lives anew to God and His ministry.

As a result of what we were sensing, my two friends began to prepare to travel with me full-time. So many doors were opening that we were often only home one week out of a month, with just enough time to regroup before heading out on the road again. The ministry was growing, and we thought we had it all figured out. We thought we knew where we were headed. Then one day the Lord told me He wanted me to become more social in my home church, because He wanted to bless me with some new relationships. As a result, I decided to accept an invitation to a wedding at our church. At the wedding, I met a wonderful woman named Kathy. As we were talking, I told her I needed an accountant for my ministry. She told me her brother was an accountant and offered to introduce us. Not long after, we all went out to dinner, and I found myself sitting across from another clue to my life destiny. Just when my friends and I had thought we had it all figured out, into my life walked this 6-foot, 4-inch man. And I married him within a year.

Suddenly, everything had changed. When we began having children a few years later, life changed even more. My life and the outworking of my calling didn't look how I thought it would, but it was God's perfect plan. Because I was relying on the help of the Holy Spirit, I could follow His clues, even through illogical seasons, toward my destiny. I never could have contrived or imagined the genius with which God has led me and prepared me through the years and seasons of my life. What a blessing it is to know that we do not have to figure it out on our own. The Helper is here to lead the way.

Help with Praying

Not only does the Holy Spirit help us find our path in life, but He helps us know how to pray. This is especially important when we face situations where we don't know how to pray. We don't know what the best outcome could be or what is needed to correct a wrong. But the Holy Spirit does. He searches the hearts of all people, and He knows the times and seasons (see Jer. 17:10; Dan. 2:21). He also knows the heart of the Father (see Rom. 8:27; 1 Cor. 2:10). In other words, though we do not always know what God's will is for a situation, the Spirit always does. When we rely on His help in prayer, He enables us to pray according to the Father's will.

One of the practical ways to pray with the Spirit's help is to pray in tongues or pray in the spirit. The ability to pray in tongues is a gift of the Holy Spirit that is available to all believers (see Mark 16:17; Acts 8:14–19; Acts 10:44–46; Acts 19:1–7). This sort of prayer arises from our spirits, not our souls. We know this because of how Paul described it: "For if I pray in a tongue, my spirit prays, but my understanding is unfruitful" (1 Cor. 14:14). Unfortunately, not all Christians believe in or value this gift from

God. Over the years, much confusion and fear has arisen around the subject of speaking in tongues. However, the Bible clearly shows us the benefit of the spiritual gift in our lives. Whole books have been written on the importance of speaking in tongues.[8] Here, we do not have the space to cover the subject fully, but we will look briefly at seven reasons why every believer should speak in tongues.

1. Speaking in tongues is the initial sign of being filled with the Spirit (see Acts 2:4).
2. Speaking in tongues is a way to worship God in the spirit (see Acts 2:11; 10:47; 1 Cor. 14:15).
3. Speaking in tongues brings spiritual edification (see 1 Cor. 14:4).
4. Speaking in tongues is a supernatural means of communication with God (see 1 Cor. 14:2).
5. Speaking in tongues reminds us of the Holy Spirit's indwelling presence (see John 14:16–17; 1 John 4:4).
6. Speaking in tongues is praying in line with God's perfect will, purpose, and order (see Rom. 8:26–28).
7. Speaking in tongues stimulates faith in God and teaches us to trust God more fully (see Jude 1:20–21).

Clearly, the gift of tongues is a great benefit to us, and all believers should embrace it and do it often. To refuse the gift of tongues is to refuse the help of the Spirit in a crucial area of our spiritual lives. One of the main passages outlining the benefits of praying in the spirit is found in Romans 8:

> So too the (Holy) Spirit comes to our aid and bears us up in our weakness; for we do not know what prayer to offer nor how to offer it worthily as we ought, but the Spirit Himself goes to meet our supplication and pleads in our behalf with unspeakable yearnings and groanings too deep for utterance. And He Who searches the hearts of men knows what is in the mind of the (Holy) Spirit (what His intent is), because the Spirits intercedes

and pleads (before God) in behalf of the saints according to and in harmony with God's will. We are assured and know that (God being a partner in their labor) all things work together and are (fitting into a plan) for good to and for those who love God and are called according to (His) design and purpose (Romans 8:26-28 AMP).

Here, Paul described praying in the spirit as the perfect way to pray for the unknown, for ourselves, and for others. This sort of prayer is free from selfishness and impure motives and, instead, is rooted in God's will. The result of this prayer is simple—the outworking of God's plan in our lives, the working of all things together for our good. Plus, when praying in tongues, our spirits are more active, and we are better able to hear God's voice. Thus, it benefits us to pray in tongues often, like the apostle Paul did (see 1 Cor. 14:18).

According to Romans 8, sometimes what the Spirit is doing in us or speaking to us is so strong that we find ourselves groaning to express it. Because these realities are spiritual and often transcend our words, we are only able to verbalize them through praying in tongues. As we do, we are declaring God's truth and will aloud, releasing them into our lives and circumstances. The more we pray like this, the more our willingness and desire to obey God will increase. This is because praying in tongues pulls upon the help of the Spirit in our lives and aligns our hearts and minds more fully with God's purposes.

Simply put, when we pray in tongues, we are praying aloud the mind, purpose, and will of God. This is important, because the Bible promises that when we pray according to God's will, He will hear us, and we will receive what we ask for:

This is the confidence we have in approaching God: that if we ask anything according to his will, he hears us. And if we know that he hears us—whatever we ask—we know that we have what we asked of him (1 John 5:14-15).

Finding Help

Thus, by praying in the spirit, we are praying prayers we know God will answer. We are praying His best prayers for our lives and situations right now with an ability that supersedes our own. What an incredible gift! Praying in the spirit also helps us discern God's will and prepares the way for His will to be accomplished in our lives. We see this principle in this prophecy from Isaiah:

> The voice of one crying in the wilderness: "Prepare the way of the LORD; make straight in the desert a highway for our God. Every valley shall be exalted and every mountain and hill brought low; the crooked places shall be made straight and the rough places smooth; the glory of the LORD shall be revealed, and all flesh shall see it together; for the mouth of the LORD has spoken" (Isaiah 40:3–5 NKJV).

Our prayers in the spirit speak forth God's will and prepare the way for His will to be accomplished, causing things to line up in the spirit first and eventually to manifest in the natural. The more we pray in tongues, the more we will be empowered to live obedient lives of surrender to God. This is what Jude referred to as building ourselves up in the faith:

> But you, dear friends, by building yourselves up in your most holy faith and praying in the Holy Spirit, keep yourselves in God's love as you wait for the mercy of our Lord Jesus Christ to bring you to eternal life (Jude 1:20–21).

The ability to pray in the spirit is an incredible gift, yet it is also a gift that requires our faith, because it bypasses our minds. Praying in the spirit is the opposite of praying with our understanding. Both are important, but especially when we do not know how to pray, we need to engage our faith and allow the Holy Spirit to help us pray the will of God. The apostle Paul talked about this in his first letter to the Corinthians:

> For anyone who speaks in a tongue does not speak to people but to God. Indeed, no one understands them; they utter mysteries by the Spirit.... For if I pray in a tongue, my spirit prays, but my mind is unfruitful (1 Corinthians 14:2, 14).

When we pray in the spirit, we do not understand what we are praying, so we must trust God that we are praying His will. To our natural selves, it may seem foolish, but the spiritual reality of praying in tongues is powerful. To benefit from the power of tongues, we must step out in faith and speak the words our minds don't understand, believing they will have impact. The more we do it, the more we will be able to sense in our spirits the power being released through our prayers. This is an essential key to our ability to live lives of surrender.

When we pray in tongues, we are praying out things we don't know or understand about God's will for our lives— things that are still a mystery to us. Whenever I need direction or sense He is doing something new or different, I pray in tongues. I am confident that I am praying according to the mind, will, and purpose of God for my life. This is how we pray when we don't know how to pray or what the future holds. Truly, the Holy Spirit is our great Helper, and when we are tuned in to His voice, we will have all we need to make the right choice on decision day. We will have the strength, courage, and wisdom to say yes to surrender and trust fully in God's will for our lives.

When we live like this, we will never be short on hope, because God is the God of all hope. In the final chapter, we will see that we can face the unknowns of surrender on decision day with hope for our future, based on the goodness of God.

Chapter 6

Embracing Hope

We live in a day when God is about to do a new thing on the earth. "Look at the nations and watch—and be utterly amazed. For I am going to do something in your days that you would not believe, even if you were told" (Hab. 1:5). God's Spirit and Kingdom are increasing on the earth. We, as His people, His bride, need to be positioned to receive all He has promised to us in these days, including a great outpouring of His Spirit. To be properly positioned, we must be people who are willing to hear His will and quick to obey. We must be people who face decision day with resolve in our hearts to trust our Father, no matter what.

When we live before Him with hearts of surrender, we have every reason to expect great things for the future. We have every reason to live in hope, because we know the one who guides our lives is infinitely trustworthy. We see this in the apostle Paul's prayer for the believers at Ephesus:

> I pray that the eyes of your heart may be enlightened in order that you may know the hope to which he has called you, the riches of his glorious inheritance in his holy people, and his incomparably great power for us who believe... (Ephesians 1:18–19).

This is the great reality of life with God, the great hope of being called by Him. But we need our minds to be enlightened (or renewed) by the Spirit to be able to comprehend it. To become people of unflagging hope, we must trust in God's perfect plan for our lives, diligently seek out our destinies along the journey of life, and believe God will work all things for our good. In this chapter, we will look at each of these keys to hope more closely.

His Perfect Plan

Like Queen Esther of old, each one of us has been called to live in our specific time in history for a reason. We entered our mothers' wombs to fulfill a unique purpose and destiny on earth—a purpose only we can fulfill. None of us are an accident, no matter the circumstances surrounding our conception and birth. God doesn't make accidents. Instead, He says, "Before I formed you in the womb I knew you..." (Jer. 1:5). Before we were conceived, God had a plan for our lives, and He picked the exact time and location in history where He wanted us to live. He has chosen each one of us to be here at this moment in history for a purpose. Paul described it like this: "In him we were also chosen, having been predestined according to the plan of him who works out everything in conformity with the purpose of his will" (Eph. 1:11).

God has a perfect plan for each of our lives. When we live surrendered to Him, we embrace His plan rather than trying to enact our own. This is wisdom, as the Book of Proverbs makes clear: "Many are the plans in a person's heart, but it is the LORD's purpose that prevails" (Prov. 19:21). When we commit our plans to the Lord, which means inviting His guidance and correction, He promises to make our plans succeed: "Commit to the LORD whatever you do, and he will establish your plans.... In their hearts humans plan their course, but the LORD establishes their steps" (Prov. 16:3, 9). This is the most certain way to success in this life—allowing God to inform our plans. When He is the author, we cannot fail.

We may fall from time to time, but the Lord will pick us up and keep us moving forward, with hope, toward our destinies in Him. David, the shepherd boy turned fugitive turned king knew all about this. At times, he must have felt like his path had become terribly confused or twisted, but he kept trusting God and following His leadership. In the end, he could testify, "The LORD makes firm the steps of the one who delights in him" (Ps. 37:23). In fact, the Bible is full of stories of people who followed God's plan for their lives when it did not make sense. They continued to trust what God had told them and look with hope-filled eyes into the future.

Hebrews 11 tells us about many of these people, like Abraham, who continued to hope for the arrival of the son God had promised him, even in his old age. Abraham actually waited twenty-five years from the time God promised him a son until the birth of Isaac (see Gen. 12:1–4; 21:5). Of course, Abraham did not always wait with perfect patience. About halfway through the twenty-five years, he and Sarah came up with a plan for how to get a son their own way. Yet, God would not accept Abraham's son Ishmael, born to Sarah's maid, Hagar. Ishmael was not the fulfillment of the promise God had planned; therefore, Abraham's plan only caused trouble in his family. So, Abraham continued to wait, and eventually he saw the fruit of his faith.

We can learn much from Abraham's example. If we are willing to believe God's plan and timing actually are perfect, we will not lose our hope for the future, even when the promise seems long in coming (or even seems as impossible as a son in old age). Waiting is not always easy, but it is better than trying to fulfill the promises of God through our own plans. Surrender is the best way forward. As Paul wrote from a Roman dungeon, "For it is God who works in you to will and to act in order to fulfill his good purpose" (Phil. 2:13). When we live like that, we will be able to say, like Jesus said, as He faced Pilate and imminent death, "… For this cause I was born, and for this cause I have come into the world…" (John 18:37 NKJV).

The Journey of Life

Once we have embraced God's plan as perfect for our lives, we get to learn how to walk that out over the course of years. Life is a journey, not a race, and God reveals our destinies to us in pieces. We discover it as we go along, living surrendered lives. If He told us the whole plan upfront, it might be a lot easier to surrender to it, but that sort of surrender would not require much faith. Because God is interested in our personal growth along the journey of life and because He wants to have a daily communion with us, He chooses, instead, to reveal our destinies in pieces. Often, He shows us the end goal—our grand calling or purpose, at least in part—but does not tell us how we will get there. He sets destiny before us, as an anchor for hope, and then He shows us how to walk one step at a time.

This means we are on a continual journey of discerning His plan for our lives, both the big picture plan and the daily plan. When we realize this, it will become one of the great joys of our lives—finding His plan for the next step and committing, yet again, to obey. This is where the prayer of dedication and consecration comes into play in our lives. When God gives us a new piece of the plan and asks us to walk forward, we face a decision day and must choose whether we will surrender or run away. Praying the prayer of dedication and consecration means saying an unequivocal yes to the next step in God's plan.

After we pray in surrender to His will, we then can ask Him questions about what it looks like to be obedient. Sometimes, it will already be clear. At other times, we will need to seek further direction: "How do I move forward from here? How do You want me to act out this decision?" As Paul pointed out, in this life, we know in part and prophesy in part (see 1 Cor. 13:12). We do not see all the details or know the full plan for our lives. We just see in part. We may have a strong sense of destiny or purpose for our lives—a bent or inclination toward a certain goal. That is just the big picture, the end goal. But the path from here to there is often unclear.

I have found that praying the prayer of dedication and consecration helps clarify and define this end goal. It helps weed out any impure motives or human desires that are not from God. Thus, the more we progress on our journey, and the more often we pray in surrender to God's will, the clearer His purpose for our lives will become. Our inner selves will rise above the struggles of our minds and emotions, and we will know in our spirits the way God is leading us. This is why the Bible refers to our spirits as the lamp of the Lord (see Prov. 20:27). Our spirits help shine His light on our inner selves and identify anything that is not of Him. When we have prayed to the point where our emotions are in check and our spirits have the right of way, we will know what God's will is. We will know how to move ahead, and we will have the strength we need to do it.

I am so glad our loving Father orders each of our steps. What a relief it is to know the wisest person in the universe has a plan for each of us! We do not need to figure out the best way forward on our own. Instead, He meets us with His gentle guiding hand every day. He is beside us in every step, leading us perfectly toward our destinies. Someone once said, "It is a mistake to look too far ahead. Only one link of the chain of destiny can be handled at a time."[9] I am glad I do not need to bear the weight and responsibility of my destiny on my own. Instead, I get to lean on the only one who knows the way there and has the strength for the task. How privileged we are to live surrendered to Him, knowing He will work all things together for our good (see Rom. 8:28).

All Things for Our Good

Some people have a hard time surrendering because they do not want to trust the outworking of their lives to anyone but themselves. They fear God will ask them to do something they don't want to or lead them into a painful situation. However, the Bible tells us God's plans for our lives are always good. Yes, struggle and pain are often a part of life on this earth, because imperfect people often hurt one another, and the enemy of our souls seeks to harm us. But God is not the one bringing pain into our lives. And He promises that when we trust Him, He is able to take even the hardest and ugliest situations and use them for our good. Only He is capable of such transformation!

Walking in surrender to His will does not mean we will never experience hardship, but it does mean we have the greatest redeemer of hardship working on our behalf. When we live in peaceful surrender, God begins to work all things together for our good. And more often than not, we will find ourselves eating the good of the land (see Isa. 1:19). As King David wrote, "The steps of a good man are ordered by the LORD, and He delights in his way" (Ps. 37:23). God's plan for our lives is the most secure place we can be. If we allow Him to order our steps, He will lead us into a delightful place.

The prophet Jeremiah famously wrote these verses that reveal God's heart for humanity:

> "For I know the plans I have for you," declares the LORD, "plans to prosper you and not to harm you, plans to give you hope and a future. Then you will call on me and come and pray to me, and I will listen to you. You will seek me and find me when you seek me with all your heart" (Jeremiah 29:11–13).

God's plans for us will not harm us. Instead, He wants to prosper us and give us a future and a hope—not only in this life but for eternity. What an incredible promise! The all-knowing and all-powerful Creator of the universe plans to prosper us and to increase our hope for the future. That means He wants to make our lives increasingly better. Throughout our lives on earth, He wants us to grow in prosperity in every area of our lives. This, of course, does not mean life will be easy. Nothing worth doing is easy. Great tasks require great strength and perseverance. But nothing is more satisfying than fulfilling God's call and walking intimately with Him. When we do that, life will be good, even if it is not easy.

Sometimes, what God leads us into might feel like it is killing us. It's like going to the gym. When we first start working out, we have a lot of under-developed muscles and extra fat that need to be addressed. At first, it will feel like we are dying. But if we persevere, our bodies will become stronger and fitter. We will lose the fat that holds us back, and our endurance will increase. The work of exercise will not be as difficult or painful, and we may even find that we enjoy it. This is what the spiritual life of surrender is like. The apostle Paul used this analogy of physical training to describe his own spiritual journey:

> Do you not know that in a race all the runners run, but only one gets the prize? Run in such a way as to get the prize. Everyone who competes in the games goes into strict training. They do it to get a crown that will not last, but we do it to get a crown that will last forever. Therefore I do not run like someone running aimlessly; I do not fight like a boxer beating the air. No, I strike a blow to my body and make it my slave so that after I have preached to others, I myself will not be disqualified for the prize (1 Corinthians 9:24–27).

Being conformed into the image of Christ is sometimes painful, especially if it involves shedding some extra baggage. But the end result will be worth it. And this is the hope we can hold onto. Christ in us is the hope of glory (see Col. 1:27). He wants to bring us to the next level of personal growth and excellence so that we can fulfill the purpose for our lives on earth. To do amazing things, we must become amazing people. This is not something we do, but something we allow Him to do in us. If we will surrender to His ways, though it may be hard and painful at times, we will discover the great goodness of His plans. We will experience what the psalmist declared:

> Many, LORD my God, are the wonders you have done, the things you planned for us. None can compare with you; were I to speak and tell of your deeds, they would be too many to declare (Psalm 40:5).

His plans for us are better than we can comprehend. As we submit to His process, He will build us into mature sons and daughters of God who do great exploits for His Kingdom. The Spirit will give us the strength we need to carry out God's plans and purposes, and we will become part of the great outworking of the gospel on earth. This is what we were made for. In a culture so focused on self-satisfaction, it is easy to forget that, ultimately, this life is not about us. It is about God and reaching this earth with the gospel message. Today is the day of God's power, and today we get to willing volunteer for His mission on earth, with our hearts filled with hope for the glorious future (see Ps. 110:3 KJV). As we are faithful to His call, we can trust His promise to give us a crown of life that never fades away (see Rev. 2:10). We can live in unhindered hope for the future, not based on our circumstances but based on His goodness. This is exactly what Paul meant when he prayed for the early believers: "May the God of hope fill you with all joy and peace as you trust in him, so that you may overflow with hope by the power of the Holy Spirit" (Rom. 15:13). This is my prayer as well. May we all be filled and overflowing with God's hope, peace, and joy as we surrender to His plans for our lives.

Conclusion

When we face the invitation to surrender on decision day, we face the close of one chapter and the beginning of another. It is like crossing over a bridge. We must step out in faith and walk across the water, trusting in our Father to hold our hands and lead us safely to the other side. His path will never let us down. He has enabled us to hear His voice, has empowered us with the indwelling presence of His Spirit, and has enlarged our vision with hope for the future. In Him, we have all we need to succeed in surrender and to fulfill our destinies in life.

In closing, please pray this prayer of dedication and consecration with me:

> Heavenly Father, I dedicate myself anew to You. I say, "Not my will, but your will be done." I only desire Your will for my life. I invite You to continue to mold me and shape me into the person You created me to be. Work in me according to Your good plan, so that I may fulfill my destiny and advance Your Kingdom on earth. Here I am, Lord. I trust You, and I say yes to whatever You ask me to do.

Conclusion

When we face the invitation to surrender on decision day, we face the close of one chapter and the beginning of another. It is like crossing over a bridge. We must step out in faith and walk across the water, trusting in our Father to hold our hands and lead us safely to the other side. His path will never let us down. He has enabled us to hear His voice, has empowered us with the indwelling presence of His Spirit, and has enlarged our vision with hope for the future. In Him, we have all we need to succeed in surrender and to fulfill our destinies in life.

In closing, please pray this prayer of dedication and consecration with me:

> Heavenly Father, I dedicate myself anew to You. I say, "Not my will, but your will be done." I only desire Your will for my life. I invite You to continue to mold me and shape me into the person You created me to be. Work in me according to Your good plan, so that I may fulfill my destiny and advance Your Kingdom on earth. Here I am, Lord. I trust You, and I say yes to whatever You ask me to do.

Endnotes

1. Chris Tomlin, Ruben Morgan, and Jason Ingram, "I Will Follow," And If Our God Is For Us, compact disc (Sparrow Records/Sixstepsrecords, 2010), track 2.

2. The Exhaustive Dictionary of Bible Names, s.v. "Gethsemane."

3. Adam R. Holtz, "Total Surrender," Pray Magazine (Nov/Dec 2011).

4. Mary Alice Isleib, Effective Fervent Prayer (Touch of Design, 1992), 60.

5. Kathryn Kuhlman, Heart to Heart (Alachua, FL: Bridge-Logos, 1998), 21.

6. The Hebrew word for restore in Psalm 23:3 and the Greek word for renew in Romans 12:2 have very similar meanings.

7. Two great books on hearing God's voice are How to be Led by the Spirit of God, by Kenneth E. Hagin, and 4 Keys to Hearing God's Voice, by Mark and Patti Virkler.

8. For more information on praying in tongues, I recommend Why Tongues by Kenneth E. Hagin, and Pray in the Spirit, by Arthur Wallis.

9. God's Little Devotional Book for Leaders (Honor Books, 2001), 124.

About Margie Fleurant

Through her keen prophetic insight, Margie is able to teach the Word of God with simplicity, precision and conviction thus bringing strength to the church. She yearns to see God's people experience success in their relationship with Him and she challenges listeners to fulfill their God given purposes here on earth.

Prayer is the cornerstone of Margie's ministry. She founded The River Ministries as a vehicle to share the importance of prayer to congregations throughout the United States and abroad.

Margie is a graduate of RHEMA Bible Training College and an ordained minister of Covenant Ministries International . She is also an ordained member of Faith Covenant Ministries.

Margie and her husband John are the parents of three grown children, Jonathan, Danielle and Jaclyn.

Other Titles by Margie Fleurant

A Love Like That

"A Love Like That" is Margie Fleurant's latest hard cover book release. This hard cover edition will increase your understanding of how much the Lord loves each one of his precious daughters.

Each one of us has a story. Our lives are like history books—with accounts of victory as well as pain, happy times and tearful times. No matter what our history has been or where we are in the progression of our story, when we encounter the love of God, we are changed. The old chapter ends, and a new chapter begins. God does not hold onto the past, but He promises to do a new thing in us. That is what this book is all about.

As you encounter God's love through the pages of this book, you will experience freshness, newness, wisdom, and increased revelation. You will discover how to be consumed with God's love, how to be changed by His perfect love, and how to continue to grow in His love throughout your life.

Discover how you can have a deeper, tender, spiritual relationship with the Lord and learn practical tips to grow closer to the Lord.

Marked for Intercession

In this book, Margie, writes from a place of authority, knowing and walking in her true calling in Christ. She is a seasoned intercessor that desires to share the Father's heart with her readers. To intercede is to "stand in the gap for those in need," and when done correctly, it is a powerful means of prayer. Margie delves into the little-known ministry of intercession; how this ministry relates to Jesus, and why it is relevant to believers today.

"It is the mission of this book is to reveal to the believer the greatest act of love, which is found in the power of persistent prayer on behalf of their families, neighbors, friends, cities and nations," "Readers will gain biblical insight into how to pray effectively."

Prayer for the Ministry Gifts

A book written specifically for ministry leaders. Church leaders need the appropriate prayer support from faithful congregants. In this book, gain insight into how the call of God effects the heart of a minister. Discover how this call motivates the leader as you prayerfully support them in fulfilling their destiny, affecting the church body as a whole.

Encounter God Through the Habit of Prayer

Many people possess a certain reverence for God, yet they view Him as a distant personality who's disinterested in the daily activities of their lives. Many are going through life unfulfilled, their spiritual hunger unsatisfied. They haven't learned the truth that God desires to walk with them in real, intimate fellowship. Learn how to experience a matchless companionship with the Lord that is anchored in prayer and vital to the human experience.

The Art of Intercession Study Guide

This is a detailed study guide for people who want to dive into God's Word and study the topic of prayer. In this booklet, readers will learn about the different kinds of prayer, the foundations needed for prayer and the power being an intercessor allows you to tap into as you pray to The Lord.

To purchase additional teaching materials or to schedule a speaking engagement, please contact Margie at:

www.MargieFleurant.org

www.ingramcontent.com/pod-product-compliance
Ingram Content Group UK Ltd.
Pitfield, Milton Keynes, MK11 3LW, UK
UKHW022221230426
12048UKWH00016BA/976